GARDENER'S DELIGHT

Gardener's Delight

JOHN SEYMOUR

with illustrations by

PETER MORTER

HARMONY BOOKS

NEW YORK

GARDENER'S DELIGHT was conceived, edited and designed by
Dorling Kindersley Limited, 9 Henrietta Street, London WC2

First published in the United States in
1979 by Harmony Books, a division of
Crown Publishers, Inc.,
One Park Avenue, New York, New York 10016

Library of Congress Cataloging in Publication Data

Seymour, John, 1914 –
    Gardener's Delight
    Includes index
    1. Vegetable gardening.   2. Cookery (vegetable).
    3. Berries.   4. Cookery (berries).
    5. Herb gardening.   6. Cookery (herbs).
I. Title
SB 322.S44 1979 635   78-24802
ISBN 0-517-53805-9

Principal sources consulted:

Banckes: *Herbal* (1525)
Boorde: *Dyetary* (1542)
Culpeper: *The Complete Herbal and English Physician Enlarged* (1649)
Evelyn: *Acetaria, a Discourse of Sallets* (1699)
Gerard: *The Herball, or Historie of Plants* (1597)
Grieve: *A Modern Herbal* (1931)
Kettner: *Book of the Table* (1877)
Lemery: *A Treatise of All Sorts of Foods* (1745)
Lovelock: *The Vegetable Book* (1972)
Parkinson: *Paradisi in Sole, Paradisus Terrestris* (1629)
Rohde: *A Garden of Herbs* (1932)
Soyer: *The Pantropheon* (1853)
Theophrastus: *Enquiry into Plants* (c. 320 BC)
Tournefort: *The Compleat Herbal, or the Botanical Institutions of
Mr. Tournefort* (1719)
Turner: *A new Herball* (1551)
Tusser: *Five Hundreth Pointes of Good Husbandrie* (1573)

Printed in Great Britain

TABLE OF CONTENTS

To the READER

AS an animal I would like to salute the vegetables! Not only does an animal's life depend upon vegetables, but most of the beauty, interest, and richness of this terrestrial globe depend on them too. I have lived in a desert and I was very glad to return to the world of plants.

How miraculous that, growing on my own little plot of land, are plants that can turn the dead soil into a hundred flavours as different as horseradish and thyme, smells ranging from stinkhorn to lavender, effects ranging from that of the foxglove – which will make your heart beat furiously and, if you eat too much of it, stop it beating altogether – to that of a tiny toadstool, which engenders splendid hallucinogenic dreams.

No wonder ancient men, set down in this Eden of plants, tentatively, and no doubt fearfully, sampling one variety after another, invested plants with magical properties. Thousands of years of plant testing, and sniffing, and tasting, and sometimes regretting it, and – yes – occasionally being sick must have passed before the great Theophrastus wrote his *Enquiry into Plants* in about 320 BC. After him came Pliny, and his contemporary Dioscorides, and many lesser classical botanists, and then the Roman civilization collapsed, and during the Dark Ages the classical lore got muddled with yet more superstition, until, come the Renaissance, William Turner revived the science of plant lore with *A new Herball* (1551). He was followed by John Gerard (1545–1612), John Parkinson (1567–1650), John Tradescant (d. *c*. 1638), Nicholas Culpeper (1616–54), John Evelyn (1620–1706), and J. Pitton de Tournefort (1656–1708) who was the greatest botanist of his time.

It is from these 16th and 17th-century plant lorists that we have drawn most of the material in this little book. Not only were they writing at the time of the greatest flowering of the English language, they were also possessed of a delicious wonderment, a freshness of vision, and a splendid naivety. They stood amazed at the richness and strangeness of the world that they were discovering, or rediscovering. With the new awareness of the classical tradition men would believe implicitly anything that they read in the writings of Greek or Latin authors. They did not doubt that Basil 'engenders Scorpions in the Braine' or that Spinach 'agrees with young people of a hot and bilious Constitution': some Roman author had told them so.

And they were not backward in inventing fantasies of their own. Culpeper, particularly, let his imagination run riot. Although he drew on the lore of the classics, it is now realized that he invented much of what he wrote. He linked every disease that the flesh is heir to with a particular phase of some star, or planet, or the Moon, and every plant also the same way;

only at the right astrological moment should it be planted, or harvested, or eaten.

Evelyn was a far more sophisticated man and we owe him an enormous debt of gratitude for his *Sylva* – a book which inspired the landlords of his time to plant trees. But his *Acetaria, a Discourse of Sallets* is the work we have drawn upon here. Parkinson treats of nearly 3,800 plants in his books, classifying them according to what he thought were their medical properties, as: 'Venemous, sleepy, or hurtful Plantes', or 'Hot and sharp-biting', and so on. Gerard was a barber-surgeon from Cheshire who set up in London and established a garden in which 'he laboured with the soile to make it fit for plants, and with the plants, that they might delight in the soil'. Things which all good gardeners should do, and we should all, every one of us, be good gardeners, for people were 'set down in a Garden to dress it and keep it' and certainly not to douse it with poisons.

De Tournefort was a serious and systematic botanist: he described every plant he knew in enormous detail. (He did not believe in the sexual life of plants – the innocence of the vegetable kingdom was as yet assumed. We now know that, like us, they get up to the *strangest* ruses to satisfy their amorous desires.)

And we come down the ages to the Frenchman who took the gastronomic world of England by storm: Alexis Soyer. He was Master Chef at the London Reform Club (and made a breakfast there for no less than two thousand people to mark Victoria's coronation), he patented a 'Magic Stove' with which a Marquis cooked himself dinner on top of the Great Pyramid, he laboured to achieve decent food in hospitals, organized soup kitchens for the poor and field kitchens for the army, and he wrote many good books on cookery.

All this may seem to have little to do with the vegetable kingdom, for Soyer's interest in plants was limited to cooking and eating them. Nevertheless he can claim to be a plant lover, as we can, for we do not eat what we do not love.

We don't have to swallow hook, line and sinker all that has come down to us from the past. In the revival (good though it is) of herbal lore a great deal of nonsense as well as sense has been foisted on us. Plants are wonderful enough *as they are* without being vested with supernatural properties. Let us accept them, take joy in them, grow them and eat them and cure ourselves with them – as the marvellous manifestations of the Life Force they truly are. We have as yet no *mineralarians* who think it sinful to eat plants as well as animals, and would have us all live on salt. Surely we can see that the Life Force intends that the less conscious (but still wonderful) organisms should nourish the more conscious – right up the chain of life. We do not do a cabbage an indignity by eating it. After all, we plant another.

JOHN SEYMOUR

MCMLXXVIII

BEETROOT

Chenopodiaceae
BIENNIAL

CULPEPER assures us that the juice of the white beet 'openeth obstructions both of the Liver and Spleen, and is good for the Head-ach and Swimmings therein, and Turnings of the Brain; and is effectual also against all venomous Creatures. . . .'As for the red beet: it 'purgeth the Head, helpeth the noise in the Ears . . . and the juice, snuffed up the Nose, helps a stinking Breath.' And more besides. The Greeks held the beet in such esteem they offered it to Apollo on silver in his temple at Delphi; today there are savants who believe that if we eat some red beet raw every day we will not get cancer. But we English normally boil the stuff for hours until it gets soft and then serve it cold, giving it, as Kettner says, a 'mawkish' taste. The Russians know what to do with beetroot; they turn it into bortsch, that most marvellous of soups. There are several other varieties of beet, from sugar beet to the huge and heavy mangold-wurzel, of which a farmer may grow sixty tons to the acre. Scientists tell us that the mangold is mostly water – to which we farmers reply: 'Yes, but what water!' For we know how the milk yield goes up, the moment we put old Fillpail on mangolds.

Beet likes well-dug, not too acid soil, with plenty of humus, and is grateful for potash – for which ordinary salt can be a substitute. Sow red beet three weeks before the last expected frost, and go on sowing successively until midsummer.

Beetroot
Beta vulgaris

Yellow beetroot

Red beetroot

SPINACH

Chenopodiaceae
ANNUAL

THE mighty Soyer, that giant of the kitchen, said of spinach: 'We only speak of the plant by way of memento, and regret that our first masters of cookery have not been able to transmit to us the results of their studies and experience in the preparation of spinach, whose precocity must always render it valuable to amateurs of food' (*The Pantropheon*, 1853). He was lamenting the fact that the Ancients, who taught us so much about other plants (much of it wrong), had nothing to say about spinach. However, John Evelyn had advised in 1699 that spinach 'being boil'd to a *Pult*, and without other Water than its own moisture, is a most excellent Condiment with *Butter*, *Vinegar*, or *Limon*, for almost all sorts of boil'd Flesh, and may accompany a Sick Man's Diet'. Spinach originally came from Persia but may have come to Northern Europe from Spain where the Arabs introduced it. Certainly when it arrived it ousted a wide range of herbs that used to be eaten as spinach is now, and this perhaps is sad, for anything that reduces variety is to be deplored. Young nettles, for example, treated like spinach in early spring, are vastly superior. But let us not decry spinach; it is most rich in vitamins A and C, iron and calcium. And there is this about it: winter and summer it is *always there*.

Spinach prefers cool weather and may run to seed in hot.
Sow it through the autumn and early spring. Hoe and
mulch, and pluck the leaves as you need them.
Spinach beet is hardier and less
likely to bolt in summer.

Spinach beet
Beta vulgaris

Spinach
Spinacia oleracea

CHICORY

Compositae
PERENNIAL

THERE has been magic attached to this plant, and a variety of legends. Dyett's *Dry Dinner* of 1599 tells us 'it hath bene and yet is a thing which superstition hath beleeved, that the body anoynted with the juyce of chicory is very availeable to obtaine the favour of great persons'. The plant grows wild in Britain, and has gone locally under such names as 'succory', 'monk's beard', 'hard ewes', 'strip for strip' and 'bunks'. Many ancient writers treat of chicory and endive together, for these two composite plants have much in common. Horace wrote about chicory being used in his time; Pliny, Virgil and Columella speak of endive. Being related to the lettuce and dandelion family, chicory has a touch of bitterness – a bitterness which can be mitigated by blanching, for the greener the leaf the bitterer it will be. Both chicory and endive are most useful to provide salads in winter, when there is little else ready for this. Chicory especially takes marvellously to forcing, and blanching, in a dark place when all else is under snow. Chicons, or white sprouts will grow. Break these off carefully as you need them and a new crop will follow. Use them fresh-picked; in the light they will droop within the hour.

Chicory likes shade, coolness, and a rich, moist soil. Sow through spring and summer for salad; sow in midsummer for forcing in winter. Weed, and keep the soil loose.

Chicory
Cichorium intybus

GLOBE ARTICHOKE

Compositae
PERENNIAL

GLOBE artichokes are under the Dominion of Venus, Culpeper tells us, 'and therefore it is no Marvel if they provoke Lust'. He then goes on to inform us that, besides being a somewhat windy Meat, 'they stay the involuntary course of natural Seed in Man' and the decoction of the root boiled in wine 'being drank, purgeth by Urine exceedingly'. Andrew Boorde, in his *Dyetary*, bears out the opinion of Culpeper concerning the aphrodisiac properties of the globe artichoke: 'they doth increase nature, and dothe provoke a man's veneryous actes.' All is not lost, though, for those who love to eat this giant thistle but have no immediate object of their affections – on the same page Boorde confides that purslane 'doth extynct the ardor of lassyvyousnes, and doth mytygate great heate in all the inwarde partes of man'. So, by judiciously cooking a little purslane with our artichokes we can enjoy the latter without risk of prosecution for immoderately passionate behaviour. As for cooking them, Parkinson says: 'The manner of preparing them for the Table is well known to the youngest Housewife I think, to be boyled in fair water, and a little salt, until they bee tender, and afterwards a little vinegar and pepper, put to the butter, poured upon them for the sauce, and so to be served to the Table.' Globe artichokes are most easily raised from suckers or offsets, which, planted in suitable soil, will just grow and grow – higher than a man.

They like rich, moist soil, and heavy mulching with manure or compost. In cold climates cut the plants down to the ground in autumn and protect them with leaves, straw or hay. Harvest when very young.

[14]

Globe artichoke
Cynara scolymus

JERUSALEM ARTICHOKE

Compositae
PERENNIAL

THIS vegetable goes under a 'gigantic misnomer', as Lovelock points out, for it has little to do with an artichoke·and nothing to do with Jerusalem. This sunflower with the swellings on the roots was called 'artichoke' because the early European settlers in America thought the tubers tasted like real artichokes (globe), and 'Jerusalem' because the Italians named all sunflowers *girasole* – the flowers gyrated towards the sun. The Jerusalem artichoke is so much like the sunflower that it is almost the same plant; the differences are that the flowers on the former and the root nodules on the latter are respectively smaller. The roots of the Jerusalem artichoke in fact taste nothing like globe artichokes, and those who have been fed too much of this vegetable may agree with John Goodyer, quoted in Gerard's *Herball*, that 'which way soever they be drest and eaten, they are a meat more fit for swine, than men'. Lovelock tells us that when the plant was introduced into England in 1616, via France from Canada where it grew wild, it was first used as a sweetmeat, but overindulgence in the making of these by pastry cooks led to it swiftly losing popularity. The root contains inulin, a substance which makes it indigestible. It has, to be fair to it, a very distinctive flavour which, when one first comes to it in a meal, can be delightful. But give me not excess of it.

They favour a light soil. Bury the tubers in the ground three to four inches deep and close enough together to smother all weeds. The better the soil, the heavier the crop – but once established, they are difficult to get rid of.

Jerusalem artichoke
Helianthus tuberosus

[17]

LETTUCE

Compositae
ANNUAL

USE of the lettuce is very ancient, it being one of those plants that, in its wild state, can be readily eaten raw and with no preparation. It is mentioned in Chinese writings of the seventh century BC. Theophrastus, writing *c.* 320 BC, describes both wild and tame varieties. Of the wild kind he says: 'It grows in fields: they extract its juice at the time of the wheat harvest, and it is said that it purges away dropsy and takes away dimness of sight and removes ulcers on the eye; for which purpose it is administered in human milk.' When Adonis died, Venus flung herself on a lettuce bed to cool her desires, and nearly every writer, ancient and modern, agrees that lettuce has that effect, allaying the 'over-violent Agitation of the Humours' (Lemery), repressing 'Venerous Dreams' (Culpeper), promoting chastity and conciliating sleep (Evelyn). Well, whatever it does, it is the basis of magnificent salad and it is perhaps the easiest plant of all to cultivate. We cannot do better than to follow Palladius' advice here: 'Lettuce delighteth to grow in a mannured, fat, moist, and dunged ground: it must be sowen in faire weather in places where there is plenty of water, as Columella saith, and prospereth best if it be sowen very thin.' We need not go to the lengths of Aristoxenus, a Greek philosopher and epicure, who 'watered' his lettuce bed with the choicest wine.

Summer and winter lettuce are best sown out of doors: spring lettuce can be started indoors in late winter, or sown out of doors and protected against frost. Hoe, water, mulch, and shade from very hot sun. Pull as you need; they don't store.

Crisphead lettuce

Cos lettuce

Loose-leaf lettuce

Red lettuce

Lettuce
Lactuca sativa

[19]

HORSERADISH

Cruciferae
PERENNIAL

THE pungent root of *Armoracia rusticana* was not used as a culinary herb in Britain in Gerard's time (1597), for he wrote that 'the Horse Radish stamped with a little vinegar put thereto, is commonly used among the Germans for sauce to eate fish with and such like meates as we do mustarde'. At that time, though, the root was used as a specific against many diseases, from dropsy to worms in children. It is still in the British Pharmacopoeia, and some modern herbalists prescribe the bruised root as a poultice or plaster, to be used as is the time-honoured and still effective mustard plaster. The slightly irritant property of horseradish is considered effective against rheumatism, now as in Culpeper's day, when that indefatigable herbalist wrote: 'If bruised and laid to a part grieved with the sciatica, gout, joint-ache or hard swellings of the spleen and liver, it doth wonderfully help them all.' Well, it doth wonderfully help roast beef. Just grate the root by rubbing it, end-grain-on, against a grater, and throw the snow-white flaky powder liberally over the cooked meat. To make the traditional horseradish sauce of Old England (albeit not older than Gerard's day): put an ounce of finely grated root in a basin, moisten with vinegar and stir into it a gill of thick cream.

Plant pieces of root in rich soil that has, ideally, some farmyard manure dug deep into it. The plant will spread; when the soil around the plants is exhausted, transplant the roots to a fresh plot.

Horseradish
Armoracia rusticana

CABBAGE

Cruciferae
ANNUAL

THE cabbage was exalted by many of the Romans – although Juvenal wrote a famous satire in which the rich patron sat down to his dish of fish garnished with olives while his wretched client was served with 'a nauseous dish' of cabbage. Pliny wrote that growing cabbages was one of the ways of supplying the table with luxuries. Apicius gives no less than five methods of preparing the cabbage: the first and simplest is to boil (but only just), pour off the water, season with cumin seed, salt, old wine, oil, pepper, alisander, mint, rue, coriander seed, gravy and – strangely – more oil. Rather than this plethora of herbal inputs I prefer the idea of 'Chartreuse'. According to Kettner, this 'looks like a dish of cabbage to be eaten by itself and for itself. But the sly monks of the Grande Chartreuse taught our cooks to hide dainty morsels of partridge within the cabbage leaves'. As for Culpeper, he surpasses himself when describing the effects of this vegetable: 'this I am sure' he says, 'Cabbages are extreme windy, whether you take them as Meat or as Medicine: yea, as windy Meat as can be eaten, unless you eat Bagpipes or Bellows, and they are but seldom eaten in our Days. . . .' A far cry from the ancient Egyptians: they not only ate the cabbage, they *worshipped* it. I confess I like it, but short of idolatry.

You can have cabbage all the year round by successional sowing and transplanting. Cabbages like good soil, with plenty of nitrogen and lime and ample watering.
In cold climates they will store well
in root cellar or clamp.

[22]

Savoy cabbage

Red cabbage

White cabbage

Cabbage
Brassica oleracea

Round-hearted cabbage

BRUSSELS SPROUTS

Cruciferae
ANNUAL

ACCORDING to Lovelock, the Brussels sprout 'positively sinks under the disdain felt for it by members of the British Commonwealth'. He goes on to tell us that the Belgians like to believe that Julius Caesar brought it to them, but that there is no evidence for this. It appears that no one is sure when the plant was brought from Belgium to England either, or who taught the English to cook it 'to the consistency of a soggy orange'. The English, I will wager a bet, did not need teaching. It would have come to them naturally. Now, there are two things to be said about the sprout. One is that *you should not boil the life out of it*. Sprouts should be dropped into briskly boiling, salted water, taken out before they are soft, drained and eaten immediately. Or – and here is something better – they can be parboiled and then roasted around the joint or tossed in boiling dripping. The second thing to be said is that *you should not have to eat sprouts all the year round*. The time to eat them is between the first frost and some point in the late winter when either the frost has destroyed them or they have grown open and blowsy and are no longer worthy of the name of sprout. True, the *tops* can be eaten after this, but the plants are better hung upside down in the hen run for the chickens.

Sprouts need firm soil, plenty of manure or compost, mulching, earthing up at regular intervals and staking when they grow very tall. When the sprouts are ready, pick them upwards along the stem.

[24]

Brussels sprouts
Brassica oleracea

BROCCOLI & CAULIFLOWER

Cruciferae
ANNUALS

DRUSUS, son of the reprehensible Tiberius, 'was so passionately fond of the brocoli, which Apicius induced him to eat, that he was more than once severely reprimanded by his father on the subject' (Soyer). When we reflect on this very father's own peccadillos, we may wonder at him finding anything very heinous in indulgence in this blameless vegetable. Indeed Soyer goes on to tell us that Glaucias 'who passed his life in meditating seriously on the perfectibility of culinary ingredients said that nothing could be better than this vegetable, boiled and suitably seasoned'. The Roman method of cooking it was to 'take the most tender and delicate parts . . . which were boiled with that extreme care the artist always devotes to this first operation; and afterwards, when the water had been well drained off, they added some cummin, pepper, chopped onions, and coriander seed – all bruised together, not forgetting, before serving up, to add a little oil and sun-made wine'. As for the cauliflower, Mark Twain called it 'but a cabbage with a college education'. Which, if it tells us nothing about the cauliflower, tells us something about Mark Twain. The cauliflower is really but a single-headed broccoli, or the latter is a many-headed cauliflower. The advantage of broccoli is that you can go on picking the flowering shoots for months (this applies to calabrese too), but the cauliflower has all its eggs, as it were, in one basket: when you have picked it, it is gone.

Broccoli will grow in most climates and most soils, but cauliflowers need care. Sow cauliflower seed indoors in early spring, successively plant out into a rich holding-bed, then into a permanent bed, and never let them go thirsty or hungry.

Broccoli
Brassica oleracea

Calabrese

Purple hearting broccoli

Purple sprouting broccoli

White sprouting broccoli

Cauliflower
Brassica oleracea

TURNIP & SWEDE

Cruciferae
BIENNIALS

EVELYN describes a sort of bread made from turnips 'which we have eaten at the Greatest Persons
Tables. . . .' You boil the turnips, press out the water,
pound the dry matter, mix an equal weight of wheat
flour with the pressed turnip, and bake in the usual
way. I have never tried this – though I will for, truly,
I cannot derive any great thrill from eating turnips in
any other way. Tournefort assures us that 'a desperate
Cough occasioned by a continual eating of lemons was
at last cured by using the Decoction of Turneps'. The
Greeks and Romans thought highly of this root – Theophrastus points out that it ran quickly to seed if a hot
wind blew – but then they had not the potato. The
arrival of the latter rather ousted the humble turnip and
swede – or at least pushed them into the cow manger
and the sheep fold where some of us might think they
belong. In Suffolk, when I was a child, a maid who
gave the brush-off to an admirer was said to have 'given
him cold turnips'. We hear the same custom from
Westphalia. In North America the Swedish turnip is
called rutabaga; this, according to Lovelock, comes
from the Swedish *rotabagge*, meaning 'red bags'. This
does not explain, however, why the Swedes came to
call them red bags in the first place.

Cultivate deeply and lime if your soil is acid, then sow seeds
of swedes and turnips where they are to grow. Thin while
they are still small. Turnips will come to
harvest about a month before
swedes.

Turnip
Brassica rapa

Yellow turnip

White turnip

Swede
Brassica napus

[29]

RADISH

Cruciferae
ANNUAL

THE radish is of ancient usage. The Egyptian pyramid builders are supposed to have eaten vast quantities, along with garlic and onions. Maybe they moved those huge stones into position with their *breath*. The Greeks esteemed it so highly that they had a golden radish in the temple at Delphi. Pliny mentions that the Romans extracted oil from radish seed but considered the root itself 'a vulgar article of diet'. Hippocrates utterly condemned the root. Evelyn tells us that radishes were 'thought to repel the Vapours of *Wine*, when the *Wits* were at their genial *Club*'. Lemery assures us that they 'drive the Stone out of the Kidneys and Bladder, and are good for the Cholic in the Back . . .' Boorde advises that they 'be not good for them the whiche hath the gowte' while Tournefort records that, according to Hoffman, if radishes be cut 'close in the wane of the Moon' they will cure corns on the feet. However Tournefort himself has 'a strong Fancy that the Medicine would work full as well, either under the Influence of the New or of the Full Moon, so that I hope no one will tie himself down to such superstitious Observances either in this or any other Case'. With which sentiments I heartily concur.

Sow the seeds in drills, in damp, rich soil, a few at a time but often, so that you have a constant supply of tender young radishes. They are ready to pick in four to six weeks.

Garden radishes

Radish
Raphanus sativus

Round white
winter radish

Round black
Spanish radish

Long white radish

Long red radish

[31]

MARROW & CUCUMBER

Cucurbitaceae
ANNUALS

FOR my part all large marrows should be reserved for the church fete, for they are good for little else. Courgettes, which are simply small young marrows, can make a pleasant, if not very nutritious addition to a meal. As for the noble cucumber, it is written of the Israelites, after they had escaped from captivity in Egypt, that they remembered 'the fish which they did eat in Egypt freely, the Cucumbers, and the Melons'. I, too, have the fondest memories of being offered sliced cucumbers in vinegar in one of the hottest places on earth. Lemery is right: the cucumber 'moistens and cools very much, quenches Thirst, allays the Sharpness of Humour, and too great Fermentation of the Blood'. It is strange that the cucumber, which probably originated in India — it is mentioned in very early Sanskrit writings, being known in that language as *soukasa* — should have achieved its highest popularity in Northern Europe. For it is the Poles and the Russians and the Scandinavians who make best use of it. They plainly do not believe (and neither do I) the theory that cucumbers are indigestible; nor do they agree (and neither do I) with Dr Johnson, who was abominably rude about this delicious fruit: 'A cucumber should be well sliced, and dressed with pepper and vinegar, and then thrown out, as good for nothing.' Fie!

Marrows and cucumbers like rich, well-drained, heavily-manured ground. They need to be well-watered but not drenched. Marrows will thrive if grown on a compost heap, cucumbers if trained up a trellis or fence. Pick courgettes when four to six inches long.

Marrow
Cucurbita pepo

Ridge cucumber

Courgette

Cucumber
Cucumis sativus

[33]

SWEET CORN

Gramineae
ANNUAL

A YOUNG man had a vision in which a beautiful fair-haired maiden appeared to him. The maiden told him to set fire to the grass of the prairie and then, catching her by the hair, drag her over the burned ground. When he did this he found that, wherever he had dragged her, maize sprang up, and that, in each ear, a tuft of the maiden's hair grew to remind him that she had not forgotten her people. There are many such legends of how maize came to the North American Indians and they indicate its importance to them. The early English settlers were kept alive by maize which they traded from the Indians; they called it 'Indian Corn' and North Americans call it corn to this day. Captain John Smith wrote: 'Their corne they rost in the eare greene and bruising it in a mortar with a Polt, lappe it in rowles in the leaves of their corne, and so boyle it for a daintie.' Francis Higginson, in *New England's Plantation*, published in 1630, wrote: 'The abundant increase of corn proves this country to be a wonderment. Thirty, forty, fifty, sixty fold are ordinary here. Yea, Joseph's increase in Egypt is outstripped here with us.' By the end of the century maize had spread around the world. The 'sweet corn' we grow in our gardens is simply maize that we pick before the grain is ripe, and boil, and eat with butter, than which there is nothing more delightful.

It needs good soil, not heavy clay, well-drained, warm, and with plenty of humus. Sow it in blocks and not narrow lines, for it is wind-germinated. Harvest when the silk has just turned brown but the grains are still milky.

Sweet corn
Zea mays

CURRANTS & GOOSEBERRIES

Grossulariaceae
SHRUBS

'SMALE raysins of Corans be good for the raynes of the backe; and they doth provoke uryne. Howbeit they be not all the best for the splene, for they maketh opylacyon.' To what fruit was Boorde referring in this very medical statement? There is great confusion about our word currant. The 'currants' we buy at the grocer shop are actually small, seedless grapes that have been dried in the sun. The name we give them is derived from Corinth, from which place many of them come. But our good British *currant* was, as Kettner points out, originally *curran*, one of the many manifestations of the old English word *cran*, which means red. We have the cranberry (red), the cranesbill (also red), the herring cran which was originally a basket of red osier, the carberry (a local name for the red gooseberry), and many other words which devolve from the root *cran* or *car*, always something red. So from *cran* we get *curran*, and then we get *currant* from a confusion with Corinth and the other 'currants'. But whatever we call them we have here the most valuable soft fruit of all. Black currants are a notable source of vitamin C, red ones make superb wine, and white currants have the virtue of being fairly unusual. Gooseberries, too, make one of the best of all country wines and take the place in our austere climate of perhaps more delicious fruit.

Currants grow well from cuttings. Gooseberries can be 'mounded': bury an old bush, except for the branch tips, in earth in summer, then gently scrape the earth away in autumn. This will reveal new roots on the branches. Cut off the branches and plant them.

Red currant
Ribes sativum

White currant
Ribes sativum

Black currant
Ribes nigrum

Gooseberry
Ribes uva-crispa

[37]

MINT

Labiatae
PERENNIAL

ACCORDING to legend mint was once a young nymph named Minthe, the daughter of a river Cocytus. Pluto made love to her and she was changed into a plant by the jealous Proserpine, and that is why mint loves damp ground near streams. There are so many varieties that the German abbot Strabo wrote, in the ninth century: 'If one wanted to tell completely all the virtues, species and names of mint, one would have to be able to say how many fishes swim in the Red Sea or the number of sparks Vulcan can count flying from the vast furnaces of Etna.' There may be in this some pardonable exaggeration but there are at least twenty species that I know of. Mint has a sort of fresh wholesomeness about it that no one can fail to delight in. Gerard says most happily: 'the smelle rejoiceth the heart of man, for which cause they strew it in chambers and places of recreation, pleasure and repose, and where feasts and banquets are made.' Culpeper allows mint to be the salvation for just about half the ills the flesh is heir to, including the bites of mad dogs. Evelyn calls it 'dry and warm, very fragrant, a little press'd, is friendly to the weak Stomach, and powerful against all *Nervous* Crudities . . .' That extraordinary poem, *The School of Salernum* has it:

> The worms that gnaw the wombe and never stint,
> Are kil'd, and purg'd, and driven away with *Mint*.

And what more can we expect it to do?

Choose a damp place, shady if you like, and simply plant some offshoots of the mint of your choice. Weed it from time to time and it will be there for years.

[38]

Common mint (Spearmint)
Mentha spicata

Peppermint
Mentha piperita

Apple mint
Mentha rotundifolia

[39]

BASIL

Labiatae
ANNUAL

'A CERTAIN Gentleman of *Siena* being wonderfully taken and delighted with the Smell of *Basil*, was wont very frequently to take the Powder of the dry Herb, and snuff it up his Nose; but in a short Time he turn'd mad and died; and his Head being opened by Surgeons, there was found a Nest of Scorpions in his Brain.' One cannot be too careful. One does not have to believe every word Tournefort wrote, although the botanical descriptions in his *The Compleat Herbal* were very sound for the time. The belief that basil bred scorpions was very widespread. This is strange because it is a pleasant-flavoured and aromatic herb, and personally I would never make turtle soup without a pinch of it. The basil is tropical and came from Asia. It is one of the sacred herbs in India, dedicated to Vishnu and Krishna. It is excellent in sausages. Among the many tales of basil is one that claims it benefits from the touch of the human hand. Old Tusser indicated that it should be planted 'trim in a pot' because gentlefolk habitually stroked a basil plant to savour the pleasant smell of it on their hands and 'such stroking from a fair lady preserves the Life of the Basil'. And Parkinson says that, far from breeding scorpions, basil has the property of procuring 'a cheerefull and merry heart'.

The plant is tender: sow the seed indoors in spring and wait until the soil outside is warm before transplanting to a well-drained, sheltered spot.

Basil
Ocimum basilicum

MARJORAM

Labiatae
PERENNIAL/ANNUALS

MARJORAM 'fortifies the Nerves', says Lemery, 'and is good for the Falling-sickness, Apoplexy, and other Distempers that affect the Brain.' Gerard thought it was 'very good against the wambling of the stomacke'. Many writers, from Pliny on, believed it was efficacious in healing wounds. I believe it is good for flavouring milk-curd and yoghurt, and also for stuffing fowls and putting in force-meats and sausages. It is wasted in soup for its flavour is fugitive; a little is pleasant in salads. Of the three kinds of marjoram that are commonly grown – Sweet, Pot, and Wild, or Oregano – the last has the sharpest, spiciest flavour and is much favoured in Italian cooking. It is strange that marjoram, which goes so well in pig-meat, should have the reputation of being abhorred by pigs. Lucretius wrote *Amaricinum fugitat sus* (swine shun marjoram), and possibly from this unproven statement came the proverbial phrase: 'as a pig loves marjoram' – in other words, not at all. It is notable in this respect that some old herbalist only had to make a statement, no matter how wild, for it to be taken as fact for ever afterwards. There are references to marjoram of some sort being grown in England from medieval times, one of them in Skelton's poem *To Mistress Marjery Wentworth* (1523):

> With Margeraine jentyll
> The flowe of goodleyhede
> Embroidered the mantel
> Is, of your maidenhede.

Pot Marjoram will grow as a perennial; strike cuttings under glass in spring and plant them out later. In northern climates Sweet Marjoram and Oregano must be grown as annuals from seed sown under glass in early spring.

Pot marjoram
Origanum onites

Sweet marjoram
Origanum majorana

Wild marjoram (Oregano)
Origanum vulgare

ROSEMARY

Labiatae
SHRUB

'THERE'S rosemary, that's for remembrance.' And like Ophelia the early herbalists thought it did indeed improve the memory. Boorde also thought it 'good for pulses, and for the fallynge sycknesse, and for the cowghe, and good agaynst colde'. Evelyn liked 'a fresh Sprig or two in a Glass of Wine'. And so do I. The name has nothing to do with roses, nor with Mary. It comes from the Latin *rosmarinus*, the 'dew of the sea'. Its flowers are the most beautiful sea-blue so we can see the reason for this. In English it was rosmarine for long – Sir Thomas More called it this when he said: 'I lett it runne all over my garden wall, not onlie because my bees love it, but because 'tis the herb sacred to remembrance, and therefore to friendship; whence a sprig of it hath a dumb language.' Certainly there is no herb that appears more in poetical literature. Besides remembrance, the herb was said to be useful in lovemaking. As it was considered to be the herb of the sea, and as Venus arose from that element, the two were connected. It was associated, too, with both weddings and funerals. Herrick wrote:

> Grow it for two ends, it matters not at all
> Be't for my bridall or my buriall.

If I don't have some sprigg'd rosemary strewed on my grave I shall haunt my posterity.

Sow seeds in spring, transplant to a holding-bed when they are six inches high, then to their permanent quarters when they are well grown. But it is easier and more reliable to plant cuttings. Pick sprigs from the second year on.

Rosemary
Rosmarinus officinalis

SAGE

Labiatae
SHRUB

EVELYN was not alone when he said of sage that 'the assiduous use of it is said to render Men *Immortal*'. 'How can a man die who grows sage in his garden?' was a much-quoted aphorism, culled originally from the *Schola Salerni*. The name comes from *salvere*, to be in good health. And not only was it supposed to make people who are already here immortal, it was also believed to bring more people here – for Lyte notes: 'Sage causeth women to be fertile, wherefore the people of Egypt, after a great mortalitie and pestilence, constrayned their women to drinke the juice thereof, to cause them the sooner to conceyve and to bring forth store of children.' Parkinson has it that sage was much used 'for teeming women; to help them the better forward in their childe-bearing'. Maybe in an overpopulated world sage is a herb to be avoided. Parkinson also, like many another writer of his time, refers to its presence in beer: 'It is also much used among other good herbes to be tunn'd up with Ale, which thereupon is term'd Sage Ale.' He specified its virtues in force-meats and stuffings as well. And here is an old recipe: Boil some pork and then mince it, mix it with an egg or two and some grated bread. Sprinkle this with salt and saffron. Roll this into a ball and wrap it in sage leaves. Wet with an egg batter, fry and serve. This was called *sawgeat*.

The old proverb holds good: 'Set sage in May and it will grow alway.' Narrow-leaved sage is better for cooking; grow it from seed. Broad-leaved sage is better for drying; grow it from cuttings.

Sage
Salvia officinalis

BAY

Lauraceae
SHRUB

BEING so resolutely evergreen the bay has always been considered a royal, a triumphant, and a god-like tree. The psalmist sang: 'I have seen the wicked in great power, And spreading himself like a green bay tree.' And who has not? Lupton, in his *Book of Notable Things* (1575), said: 'Neyther falling sickness, neyther devyll, wyll infest or hurt one in that place where a bay tree is.' Culpeper reiterates this: 'Neither witch nor devil, thunder nor lightening, will hurt a man where a bay tree is.' The tree had magical properties – it was a widespread belief that you would never be struck by lightning while standing by a bay tree and, in all truth, I am forced to admit that in a long life I never have been. But it was an evil omen, often signifying death, for a bay tree to die. Witness the Welsh captain's words in Shakespeare's *Richard II*:

> 'Tis thought the king is dead; we will not stay.
> The bay trees in our country are all wither'd.

The bay tree was formerly called the laurel – bay comes from the French *baies* meaning berries. As is well known, the laurel was held in great esteem by both ancient Greeks and Romans. Victors were crowned with it, the priests of Apollo wore it on their heads, diviners and prophets carried it to increase their powers, and young girls burned the leaves to bring back errant youths.

If you grow bay in a northern climate, plant it in a tub so that it can be taken indoors when frost or harsh winds threaten. Pick the leaves all year – but dry before cooking with them.

Bay
Laurus nobilis

RUNNER BEAN

Leguminosae
ANNUAL

RUNNER, French and Dwarf beans are really one and the same thing, simply specialized varieties of *Phaseolus vulgaris*. Before Columbus the Old World knew not *Phaseolus* – nor the New World *Vicia*, the Broad bean of Europe. The Aztecs, although they knew so much about building, human sacrifice, and the calendar, did not keep domestic animals; for their protein the people ate beans of the *Phaseolus* genus (*P. vulgaris* and *P. limensis*, the lima bean). The conquistadors brought *P. vulgaris* back to Spain, from where it spread to Britain. The Runner bean was brought in first as a flower, but soon people discovered how good it is to eat. Now there are three ways of eating beans. The first is pods and all, with the seeds still immature (thus we eat Runner beans); the second is the seed alone, tender and unripe but out of the pods (thus we eat Broad beans); the third is the seed quite ripe, quite dry and stored for the winter or other times of scarcity. Such dried pulses can be ground to powder, kibbled or cracked, or just soaked in water and boiled. I would enjoin the gardener to eat his fill of Runner beans and French beans while they are still tender and green, in the pods. Then, when the productivity of these marvellous plants defeats him, he should leave the pods on the vines to get quite ripe, pull the vines, hang them in a shed, thrash them out in the winter, and store. A pot of *Haricots à la Portugaise* will keep the cold out like nothing else.

They are not frost-hardy so sow the seed after the last frost.
They love humus, and plenty of moisture at their roots. Give
them tall enough stakes and they will grow
twice the height of a man.

Runner bean
Phaseolus vulgaris

PEAS

Leguminosae
ANNUALS

PEASE 'poredge' or pudding was once a standby of the country people of England, and should be again, for the common pea grows well in the British climate, crops heavily, is high in protein, and very good to eat. Further, pease pudding is made of dried peas, which will keep. It was eaten much in Lent as a vegetable-substitute for forbidden meat – 'Pease pudding hot, pease pudding cold, pease pudding in the pot four days old'. Until Tudor times peason (which is the correct plural of pea) were always eaten dried; then the practice of eating them green and fresh came and now many people never taste them in any other way, which is sad, for dried and suitably cooked with bacon or pork, they are marvellous. Tusser wrote a verse to the point:

> Good peason and leekes, to make poredge in Lent
> And peascods in July, save fish to be spent.
> Those having, with other things, plentifull then
> Thou winnest the love of the labouring men.

But Parkinson is most undemocratic: peas, he says, 'are either used when they are green, and be a dish of meat for the table of the rich as well as the poor, yet everyone observing his time, and the kind: the fairest, sweetest, youngest, and earliest, for the better sort, the later and meaner kinds for the meaner . . . Or, Being dry, they serve to boyl into a kind of broth or pottage . . . much used in Town and Country in the Lent-time, especially of the poorer sort of people.'

St David's and St Chad's days – March 1 and 2 – are traditionally recommended for sowing peas; you can go on sowing successially until July if you plant early varieties. Sow them thickly in well-mucked ground and give them sticks to grow up.

Peas
Pisum sativum

[53]

BROAD BEAN

Leguminosae
ANNUAL

THE Broad bean is what bean feasts were made of, and the bean feast has a very ancient history, for it was common in antiquity to have a feast with beans after a funeral. But there were also many sinister beliefs attached to this vegetable, one of the more foolish being that the spirits of the dead resided in it. Pythagoras believed this and would on no account eat beans; the Egyptians regarded them with horror, as unclean. The Romans had a proverb, *abstineto a fabis* – abstain from beans – but this was derived from their method of voting by casting beans into a bowl and it was simply an injunction to have nothing to do with politics. The reasonable Kettner, after mentioning some of the above prejudices, concludes with a sound moral: 'Two thousand years pass by, and here we are now eating beans with the most thorough enjoyment and the most perfect unconcern. Moral – Get rid of prejudice and call nothing unclean.' However it is not just the edible part of the bean which has provoked dark thoughts; the bloom has too. The very richness of the scent has given rise to several superstitions, including one which has it that to sleep in a bean field causes madness. I prefer James Thomson's assessment of this splendid aroma:

> Long let us walk
> Where the breeze blows from yon extended field
> Of blossomed beans. Arabia cannot boast
> A fuller gale of joy that liberal thence
> Breathes through the sense and takes the ravished soul.

Sow them in the autumn – and let them weather the winter – so they get away quickly in the spring and beat the blackfly. If you delay until spring, then sow very early – 'when elm leaves are as big as a farthing'.

[54]

Broad bean
Vicia faba

LEEK

Liliaceae
PERENNIAL (grown as ANNUALS)

ALL good husbandmen eat leeks in Lent, in fact all through the 'hungry-gap' in spring, when fresh vegetables are at a premium. The hardy leek stands the winter and grows on in the spring. The older writers believed all sorts of wonders of this stalwart of the Lily family. Lemery, after attributing some rather indelicate properties to it, tells us that it 'stops Vapours, and prevents Drunkenness: It is externally applied for the stinging of Serpents, Burnings, Emrods . . . and the Juice they use for to cure Noise in the Ears'. Maybe it is its effect on Drunkenness that causes my Welsh neighbours to be such sober fellows. The Reverend Hilderic Friend, in his *Flowers and Flower Lore*, explains how the Welsh came to adopt this splendid plant for their emblem. He quotes an ancient author who claimed that in the year 640 the Britons under Cadwallader won a victory over the Saxons 'by the judicious regulation [St David] adopted for rendering the Britons known to each other, by wearing Leeks in their caps . . . while the Saxons, from the want of such a distinguishing mark, frequently mistook each other, and dealt their fury among themselves'. And a good Welshman still, in the words of Fluellen, 'takes no scorn to wear the leek upon Saint Tavy's Day' for it is an 'honourable padge'. Evelyn, however, says of leeks: 'The Welch, who eat them much, are observ'd to be very fruitful.' I don't know what we may deduce from that.

To grow fair leeks — neither too large nor too mean — sow the seed in a fine seed-bed in early spring, transplant to a holding-bed of rich soil in early summer, and then to a permanent bed in midsummer.

[56]

Leek
Allium ampeloprasum

[57]

ONION

Liliaceae
PERENNIAL (grown as ANNUALS)

GERARD gives hope for those of us whose heads appear more suited for the housing of brains than the growing of hair: 'the juice [of Onions] annointed upon a pild or bald head in the Sun, bringeth the haire again very speedily.' Boorde tells us that onions incline us towards dalliance. Herein lies a contradiction – they would incline us to do what the aroma they impart to our breath (or our heads, if we believe Gerard) would make more difficult. It is true that onions have always aroused strong passions. Some people hate them, some adore them. Alexander the Great fed them to his troops because he believed they increased their martial ardour. Brahmins and holy men in India eschewed the plant because they believed it mitigated against calmness. Onions have the reputation of guarding against contagious diseases, for their juices are antiseptic; well boiled in milk they are a remedy for colds. And some say that good cooking means using plenty of onions – or members of the onion tribe. Spring onions are just immature onions; in other words, they do not pack the same gate-slamming power. As for eating onions – here is my recipe. Sit down under an oak tree and spread a white-spotted red handkerchief on your lap. Place on it a hunk of wholemeal bread, a hunk of cheese, and a raw onion. Pull out your pocketknife, cut off mouthfuls from each of these three articles of sustenance, and put them in your mouth. Wash them down with home-brewed beer.

The cultivation of onions has lost much of its mystery with the introduction of onion sets. Older gardeners who think they 'know their onions' do not use them, but grow from seed; sow this in late summer, in a seed-bed, and plant out in spring.

Onion
Allium cepa

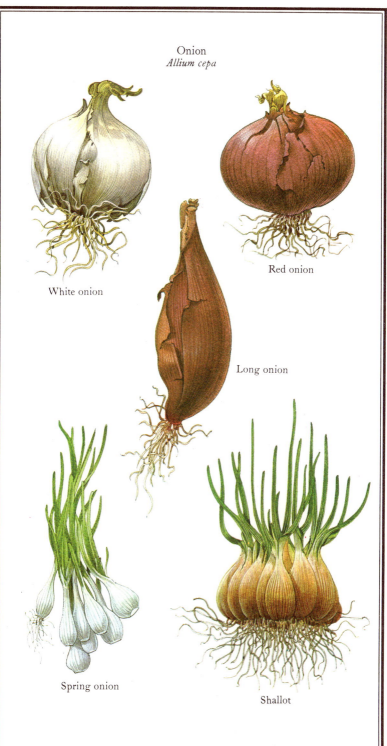

White onion

Red onion

Long onion

Spring onion

Shallot

GARLIC & CHIVES

Liliaceae
PERENNIALS

SIR John Harrington, in his *English Doctor* of 1609, wrote:

> Sith Garlicke then hath power to save from death,
> Beare with it though it makes unsavory breath;
> And scorne not Garlicke, like to some that think
> It onely makes men winke, and drinke, and stinke.

How sad that books of medicine and other learned works are no longer written in quatrains. The over-fastidious English have always been inclined to shy away from this delectable bulb. Thus Evelyn: 'We absolutely forbid it entrance into our Salleting, by reason of its intolerable Rankness. To be sure, 'tis not for Ladies Palats, nor those who court them. . . .' For my part I like to eat some garlic every day of my life; it is undoubtedly the most beneficial plant for the human health. Lucas, in *Nature's Medicines*, has it that it cures everything from worms to consumption. Grated it has been successfully applied, by the Russians, to open wounds, and I know a lady who claims she feeds it to her cows to cure them of mastitis. As for the humble chive, it is a charming thing to grow as edging to a garden and, because it is a monocotyledon, you can cut and come again. Chives share this property with grass: the leaves grow from their bases and therefore the grazing off of their tips does not damage them. I chop up some chives to mix in the mash that I give to young poultry and it does them good.

Plant garlic cloves in autumn or spring, in good, rich soil and a sunny spot. Keep them free of weeds. Sow chives from seed or, better, from a borrowed clump in spring or summer. Make sure they have plenty of moisture.

Chives
Allium schoenoprasum

Garlic
Allium sativum

[61]

ASPARAGUS

Liliaceae
PERENNIAL

THERE are said to be about one hundred and twenty species of this close relative of the lily of the valley, one of which labours under the name of *Asparagus horridus*. Something looking very much like the plant is depicted on Egyptian murals of the third millennium BC, so it is not a new plant. The Greeks used it for medicine and the Romans, who knew a good thing to eat when they saw one, indulged themselves on it. They knew, too, not to overcook this vegetable, for Suetonius, describing an over-hasty action of Caesar Augustus, said he performed it: '*citius quam asparagus coquantur*' – quicker than cooking asparagus. Asparagus was originally a sea-marsh plant and it is still to be found in a wild state in some saltings. The cultivation seems to have died out in Europe with the fall of the Roman Empire, but was re-introduced by the Arabs in the late Middle Ages. It is mentioned in French writings of 1469 and in English in 1538. Now it is esteemed as a great luxury and is flown to Europe at all sorts of unseasonable times from the sunny Americas. This is a pity, for it jades the palate and we fail to enjoy that great pleasure in May when asparagus comes, with the cuckoo, to bring us joy.

Asparagus prefers a light or sandy soil, enriched with manure. Plant three-year-old roots, taking care not to let them dry out before planting. You can start cutting in the second year and then go on cutting, perhaps for a decade. But don't cut after Midsummer's Day.

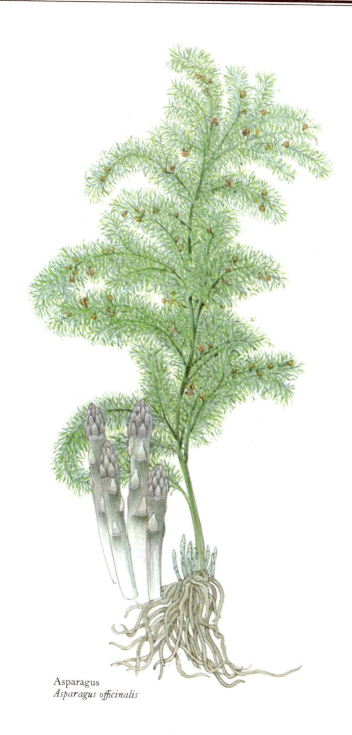

Asparagus
Asparagus officinalis

RHUBARB

Polygonaceae
PERENNIAL

WE CLASSIFY rhubarb as a 'fruit' in gastronomic terms simply because it is rich in acid. The part of the plant that we eat, of course, is not a fruit at all but a stem. And it is not of ancient usage as a dessert in Europe. One of the first commercial growers of this plant in England, Joseph Myatt of Deptford, sent five bunches of the stems to the Borough Market in 1810 and had to take two of them back because they were not known or wanted. He persevered however, and gradually people got to know rhubarb and like it; at first some made the mistake of trying to eat the leaves, boiled, like spinach, and there were those who died. This experience should not put us off the stems though. Long before these were eaten in Europe the roots reached us from the Orient to be used as medicine. Tournefort called the plant *Rhabarbarum*, 'a word importing a Root which grows among barbarous Nations: for 'tis found near the River *Rha*, known by the name *Wolga* in *Moscovy*'. Grieve gives us this derivation too, but adds that some authorities derive the name from the Greek *rheo* – to flow – in allusion to the plant's purgative properties, which, in the days before antibiotics, were especially useful in the treatment of bacillary dysentery. I use rhubarb for making summer wine – of all the plants from which we can make this in northern latitudes, it is probably the best.

Plant a rooted crown in deeply-dug, well-manured soil. When established, cover the plants with upturned pots or buckets, to force them in the spring. To harvest, pull (don't cut) the stems, and never take more than half from a plant in one picking.

Rhubarb
Rheum rhabarbarum

STRABERRY

Rosaceae
PERENNIAL

'RAWE crayme undecocted, eaten with strawberys or hurtes is a rurall mannes banket. I have known such bankettes hath put men in jeopardy of they lyves.' Rural men must have been able to afford more strawberries in Boorde's day than we can now. We can *grow* them all right, but the temptation is to sell most of them. And as for over-indulgence in strawberries and cream putting a man in jeopardy of his life – well, what a glorious way to die. Sooner or later, when discussing strawberries, everybody comes up with that felicitous quotation: 'Doubtless God could have made a better berry, but doubtless God never did', but few people seem to know from whom it derived. Many plump for Dr Johnson. In fact, it came from another doctor – William Butler – and is quoted by Walton in the *Compleat Angler*: 'We may say of angling as Dr Boteler said of strawberries. . . .' Our strawberries have been made what they are – fat and luscious – by the admixture of two strains from the Americas, *Fragaria chiloensis* from the west coast and *Fragaria virginiana* from the east. Our own indigenous berries – the little wild wood strawberries, which flower along the lanes around my farm – are *Fragaria vesca*, and it was surely to these that Gloucester was referring in Richard III when he said to the Bishop of Ely:

> When I was last in Holborn
> I saw good strawberries in your garden there.

Obtain some good, virus-free runners from a reliable nursery, plant in late summer in well-manured ground, water and weed well, and replace after three years.

Strawberry
Fragaria x Ananassa

RASPBERRY

Rosaceae
PERENNIAL

RASPBERRIES, in Lemery's opinion 'were proper in warm weather, and suit young bilious People, and such in whom the Humours are too sharp, and over-much agitated.' I find that the young people on my farm, whether bilious or not, make a bee-line for the raspberry canes as soon as these come into bearing. Now raspberries are sublime with thick cream, and also make fine wine. Parkinson mentions raspberry wine as being a common article of trade: 'It is generally held of many . . . that the red wine that is usually sold at the Vintners, is made of the berries of Raspis that grow in colder countries, which give it a kind of harshnesse. . . .' The best raspberries come from Scotland. The leaf of the raspberry is also valuable. Raspberry leaf tea is still used by many country people. Pregnant ladies drink it, believing it good for them; it is good for counteracting over-activity of the bowels, fine as a mouth-wash or as a gargle for sore throats, and a good wash for wounds or ulcers. Tusser liked the raspberry and, being a believer in companion planting, wrote:

> The barbery, respis, and goosebery to,
> looke now to be planted, as other things do:
> The goosebery, respis, and roses al three,
> with strawberries under them, trimly agree

Maybe he would not have advocated the planting of the barberry if he had known that this bush was the alternative host of *smut* in wheat, a disease which has caused famines in its time.

Raspberries put out suckers. Dig these up, with some roots attached, and plant in good soil — preferably slightly acid — with plenty of manure. Don't let them fruit the first year; remove the blossoms.

Raspberry
Rubus idaeus

BLACKBERRY

Rosaceae
PERENNIAL

WHEN Satan was expelled from Heaven he fell into a blackberry bush. He was ejected on October the eleventh – Michaelmas Day according to the Old Calendar – and since that time he comes up from below every year on that day to curse the blackberries. That is why, after that date, the fruit is not fit to eat. It is tasteless and mushy, often covered with 'cuckoo-spit', and he who eats of the berries shall not only be disappointed by their taste but he shall also, traditionally, have bad luck. Before that time blackberries are the most delicious of fruit – and none the worse because they are free. As Whitman wrote: 'the running blackberry would adorn the parlours of heaven'. And the Highlanders call it *an druise beannaichte* – the bramble blessed – and have considered it a sovereign remedy against many ills, including devils. It really does seem to have been a specific against burns, and sores in the mouth, and other ulcers. Tusser advocates the sowing of bramble seeds. In his day, when men enclosed the commons, they ploughed a wide strip around the land they were enclosing and planted this with bramble, hips, haws or whitethorn, and hazel nuts. The result was a hedge which not only kept stock in – or out – but also provided much good food. We were the beneficiaries of this until the bulldozer ripped so many of the hedges out and now many children never have the joy of blackberrying in the late summer.

Propagate by cuttings, suckers or layering in well-drained soil in a sheltered spot. Prune in winter after they have fruited, and mulch plentifully.

Blackberry
Rubus macropetalus

CAPSICUM

Solanaceae
PERENNIAL (grown as ANNUALS)

CHRISTOPHER Columbus, no less, was the first person to import the capsicum into the Old World, and in so doing started off one of those linguistic confusions which bedevil gardeners. For, because capsicums tasted 'hot' people called them 'peppers'; but the pepper (*Piper negrum*) comes from an entirely different natural order, the *Piperaceae*, and grows on vines on the Malabar Coast of India. The capsicum was cultivated in Central America as early as 7000 BC; there are many varieties, not all of them hot. Some such as the large 'bell peppers' are mild enough to be eaten green and unripe; others such as the long pepper, cone pepper, red cluster pepper and the chilli are, as Evelyn warns, 'of dangerous consequence with us; being so much more acrimonious and terribly biting quality'. It would be intriguing to know what Indian cooking – which depends so strongly on the chilli – was like in pre-Columbian times, before the Portuguese carried the plant to India in the 16th century. There, according to Clusius in his *Exoticorum* (1605), it was cultivated under the name of Pernambuco Pepper. About the same time Gerard tells us that capsicums were 'very well knowne in the shoppes at Billingsgate by the name of Ginnie pepper'. We may suppose that the many members of the capsicum tribe spread so widely through the world partly because of their flavour but also because they are one of the richest sources of vitamin C.

As tropical fruits they need a temperature of at least 65°F (18°C) or they will not set fruit. You will get a better crop under glass. Treat them like tomatoes: plant deeply, mulch heavily, water well when young but always the roots, never the peppers.

Pepper
Capsicum annuum

Chilli pepper

TOMATO

Solanaceae
PERENNIAL (grown as ANNUALS)

'APPLES of Love', tomatoes were called by the old herbalists, who attributed all sorts of potency to them once they had conquered their reluctance to swallow them at all. For long after the Spaniards brought them from Peru they were grown only as an ornamental plant, considered to be poisonous. But by Gerard's day, they were accepted, reluctantly, as at least being edible: 'In Spaine and those hot Regions they eat the Apples prepared and boiled with pepper, salt, and oyle: but they yeeld very little nourishment to the body, and the same naught and corrupt.' Gerard believed 'a great coldnesse' was contained in the plant 'which I leave to every mans censure'. The North Americans — who acquired the tomato from England — took even longer to discover that it was palatable: they have made up for it since, though. Our name for this berry derives from the Aztec *tomatl*, but the plant originated in Peru; we know they had the tomato in 500 BC. The first seed to come to Europe travelled by caravel to Spain and then was planted in Morocco. When it reached Italy it was called *pomo dei mori* — apple of the Moors. Later this was corrupted to *pomo d'ore*, and this was anglicised to 'Golden Apple'. Which it was called until our lusty English botanists — ever ready to attach amorous powers to any strange-looking plant — changed it to 'Apple of Love'.

Tomatoes love sun and hate frost. Sow thinly in compost under glass in a well-drained, sunny position. Plant out in the first warm weather. Water diligently, hoe and mulch within reason, and allow to set about four trusses.

Tomato
Lycopersicon lycopersicum

Pear tomato

Yellow tomato

Continental tomato

AUBERGINE

Solanaceae

PERENNIAL (grown as ANNUALS)

THE French word *aubergine* can be traced back to
the Sanskrit *vatingana*; this became *badin-gan* in
Persian, *badinjan* in Arabic, *alberengena* in Spanish. The
fruit itself was certainly cultivated in very early times in
India. It may have been bred up from *Solanum insanum*
or from *Solanum incanum*, both natives of that sub-
continent. The plant was not known to the ancient
Greeks or Romans, but apparently worked its way here
via the Arab world, North Africa and the Iberian Penin-
sula. It is now a vegetable *par excellence* of the Medi-
terranean area, where it does excellently. Like all
solanaceous plants it has a slightly sinister tradition
attached to it. Most of the members of this, the deadly
nightshade family, are poisonous in part at least: the
immature fruit of the aubergine contains too much of
a poison called solanine to be good for us (and so do
the leaves and stems). Like the other members of this
family, too, except the humble potato, there is a conno-
tation of luxury attached to it – almost of a tropical
decadence. One Turkish dish of aubergines is called
Imam Bayeldi, which means 'Swooning Imam'. The
Imam in question was so overcome by the glorious
taste of this dish when it was served to him by his un-
veiled concubines, that he passed right out. The old
English name was 'Raging Apple' or 'Mad Apple'.
Gerard warns darkly: 'doubtless these Apples have a
mischievous qualitie, the use whereof is utterly to bee
forsaken.' Advice which I shall hasten to ignore.

*Sow seed in peat pots in an unheated greenhouse and plant
out in deeply-dug, well-manured, rich loam after all danger
of frost has gone. Water well and protect
with cloches until the warm
weather comes.*

[76]

White
aubergine

Aubergine
Solanum melongena
var. esculentum

POTATO

Solanaceae
ANNUAL

THE potato was cultivated by the inhabitants of Peru at least as early as 750 BC. However, it reached North America, not from the South, but via Ireland. Sir John Hawkins brought the plant to Ireland from South America in 1565, in 1585 Sir Francis Drake took it to England, and not until much later was the plant introduced into North America – to Virginia – from potatoes that had been grown in Ireland. It took time to be accepted in Europe – although it was early eaten and high prices paid for it – because it was supposed to be an aphrodisiac (Falstaff cried 'Let the sky rain potatoes!' when he wished for vigour to tackle the Merry Wives). For long the general run of people thought the potato poisonous. This was no doubt because they tried eating the tops, which are poisonous, and also the tubers after they had been exposed to the light, when these turn green and bitter and become poisonous too. Many would not eat the potato because it is not mentioned in the Bible and a rumour spread that it engendered leprosy. The Irish grew potatoes extensively for the simple reason that they could be left in the ground until needed and therefore could not be seized as rent by the agent of the landlord. This individual could (and did) raid the barn and carry away all wheat, barley and oats but he could not demean himself by grubbing about in the ground to dig potatoes.

Plant the tubers in plenty of muck, or compost, or seaweed, or comfrey leaves, after the last frost. Ridge them up as needed, and spray with Bordeaux mixture if there is a blight warning. Be sure to keep them free of weeds.

Potato
Solanum tuberosum

[79]

DILL

Umbelliferae
ANNUAL

I KNOW of two noble uses for dill. The first is the dill barrel. This is a barrel full of pickled gherkins and dill tops and seeds. There is just nothing you can do in the presence of such an object but *keep eating*. Evelyn testifies to this, being particularly partial to 'Gerckens muriated with the seeds of Dill'. To fill a dill barrel, or crock, put in alternate layers of gherkins or ridge cucumbers and dill – the ripe tops of the plants are best – and, when full, pour in a concentrated cold brine. Put a scrubbed board with a stone on it to keep it down. The other noble use for dill is the famous gripe-water that many a father drinks, diluted with gin, when it is his turn to get out of bed to attend to his crying baby. The gripe water (without the gin) is of course a traditionally soothing remedy for infants; it 'destroyeth the yexing' (hiccoughs), as Banckes wrote. The word dill comes from the Norse *dilla*, meaning 'to lull to sleep'. Presumably this is why dill seeds were also called Meeting House seeds; they were taken by long-suffering congregations to allay the tedium of particularly dreary sermons. Dill was once much used in medicine. Culpeper says that, besides being 'a gallant expeller of wind', the roasted seed was good against ulcers, 'especially in the Fundament'. Another excellent use of the herb is dill vinegar, which gives a splendid flavour to salads.

Sow seeds successively through spring and summer for a constant supply of dill. It needs sun, watering, and well-drained soil. Before threshing the seed heads be sure to dry them, in a temperature not above blood heat.

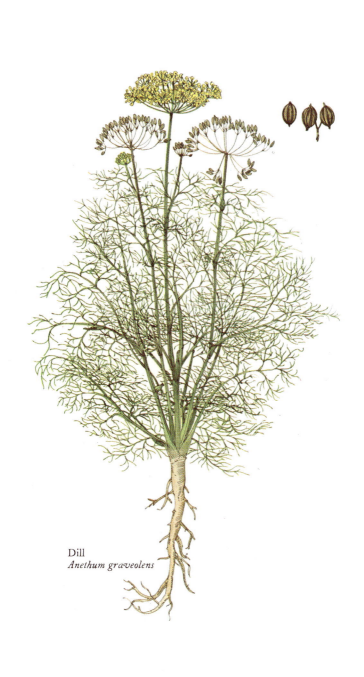

Dill
Anethum graveolens

ANGELICA

Umbelliferae
BIENNIAL

THIS acquired its angelic name from the supposition that it first blooms every year on the day of Michael the Archangel (which used to fall on the eighth of May). I have to admit that my specimen seldom lives up to its name. Probably because the Saint was so successful in casting the Devil out of Paradise, this herb has been used to ward off witchcraft and other evils:

> Contagious aire, ingendring pestilence
> Infects not those that in their mouths have ta'en,
> Angelica, that happy Counterbane.

Thus Guillaume du Bartas, translated in the 17th century by Joshua Sylvester. Well, whether it defeats the Devil or not, it is a delicious herb. Chartreuse is flavoured with it, and so is Vermouth. The Icelanders eat the stems and roots of it raw, and the Laplanders, who believe that it strengthens life, chew it as less sensible people chew tobacco. They used to crown their poets with it. And of course, candied, angelica is delectable. 'The whole plant', wrote Parkinson, 'both leafe, roote, and seede, is of an excellent comfortable sent, savour and taste.' As for Culpeper, he raved about its curative properties. It was efficacious, he declared, in the treatment of: Poison, Pestilence, epidemical Diseases, Cholick, Wind, Pleurisy, Cough, Lungs, Breast, Strangury, Shortness of Breath, After-Birth, Stoppings of the Liver and Spleen, Indigestion, Surfeits, Toothach and the Bitings of mad Dogs.

Angelica is winter hardy and is a suitable subject for shady positions. It will grow from seed in a good, deep loam. Pick the leaves and leaf stalks in early summer; dig up the roots in the second autumn of the plant's life.

Angelica
Angelica
archangelica

CELERY

Umbelliferae
BIENNIAL

THEOPHRASTUS mentioned it, so did Pliny, and Apicius – that male forerunner of Mrs Beeton – recommended it constantly for flavouring. But celery did not apparently reach the British Isles until Tudor times. Evelyn, writing in the late 17th century, says it 'was formerly a stranger with us (nor very long since in Italy), is an hot and more generous sort of *Macedonian Parsley*, or *Smallage*. The tender leaves of the *Blancht* Stalk do well in our Sallet, as likewise the slices of the whitened Stems, which being crimp and short, first peel'd and slit long wise, are eaten with *Oyl*, *Vinegar*, *Salt*, and *Peper*; and for its high and grateful Taste, is ever placed in the middle of the *Grand Sallet*, at our Great Mens Tables and *Praetors* Feasts, as the Grace of the whole Board.' In olden times celery was much used medicinally and was held to cure a great many ills. It happens to be rich in certain minerals, and also vitamins. Nowadays we are apt to throw away the green tops and eat only the blanched stalks; however if you dry the green tops and use them as a herb to flavour stews, you will benefit – for the vitamins reside more in the green leaves than in the whitened stems. Celery seed also used to be a common flavouring for stews when I was a boy; now one seldom sees it, which is a pity, for it imparts a quite delicious flavour.

Start celery indoors in seed boxes; keep the seedlings moist but not sodden. Prick out the plants, then put them in trenches well enriched with manure. Never let them dry out. Earth them up as they grow, to blanch them.

[84]

Celtuce

Celery
*Apium graveolens
var. dulce*

Self-blanching celery

CORIANDER

Umbelliferae
ANNUAL

ONE of the many joys of eating good Indian food is biting into the occasional coriander seed and experiencing a little explosion of flavour in the mouth. Coriander has long been esteemed in the East; it is also one of the bitter herbs ordained to be eaten at the Passover. English herbalists, it is almost needless to say, thought that it 'stimulated the passions' (Robert Turner, in his *Brittish Physician*). However, English children have traditionally been able to buy little comfits made from sugar-coated coriander seeds. What effect these have had on their passions we do not know, but consumed in quantity the seeds are a narcotic. Coriander has certainly featured in the distilling of gin and in the flavouring of liqueurs. The Greeks and Romans both used it – the latter to spice a vinegar which they poured over meat to act as a preservative. Lemery tells us that coriander 'sweetens a stinking Breath', Gerard that it 'easeth the squinancie'. And Grieve, in her *Modern Herbal*, tells of an old family recipe for 'Lucknow' curry powder: '1 oz ginger, 1 oz coriander seed, 1 oz cardamum seed, $\frac{1}{4}$ oz best Cayenne powder, 3 oz turmeric. Have the best ingredients powdered at the druggist's into a fine powder and sent home in different papers. Mix them well before the fire, then put the mixture into a wide-mouthed bottle, cork well, and keep it in a dry place.' I tried this, powdering the ingredients in a pestle myself, and the resulting curry transported me back to India.

Sow the seed in late spring. After flowering and when the seeds turn brown, pull the plants out of the ground and hang them up to dry. Dry the seed thoroughly before using or it will be bitter to the taste.

Coriander
Coriandrum sativum

CARROT

Umbelliferae
ANNUAL

'ALL the sorts being boyled in the broth of beef, either fresh or salt, but more usually of salted beef, are eaten with great pleasure, because of the sweetness of them: but they nourisheth less than Parsnips.' And in the latter statement Parkinson was right; Sir Humphrey Davy calculated that potatoes are the most nutritive of our roots and tubers, parsnips second, and carrots third. Carrots were eaten in antiquity – probably wild ones. Pliny and Columella mention them. The wild carrot was preferred by herbalists to the cultivated type. Lemery tells us: 'They are sudorifick, good for Wounds, opening, proper for the Stone and help Womens Terms.' Most old writers thought they inclined to amorousness – Boorde writes: 'Caretes soden and eaten doth auge and increase nature, and doth cause a man to make water.' Gerard mentions them as 'serving for love-matters', and Lehner, in *Folklore of Odysseys*, says that the Greeks called the carrot *philon*, from *philo* (loving). 'Its root', he writes, 'was served as a vegetable before amatory affairs because it was believed to possess the power of exciting the passions. It was also believed that raw carrots improve the eyesight.' There is some evidence to support the eyesight theory, and modern herbalists do. In the Second World War it was put about that British night fighter pilots were successful because they were fed largely upon carrots. They *were* fed largely on carrots, but it was radar that enabled them to shoot down aeroplanes in the dark.

Evelyn tells us that carrots should be 'rais'd in Ground naturally rich, but not too heavy' and in this he was right. Light, even sandy, soil, well-dunged for a previous crop, is good for them; fresh dung makes them fork.

Carrot
Daucus carota

FENNEL

Umbelliferae
PERENNIAL/ANNUAL

THE fennel is a magnificent looking plant and an embellishment to any garden. Although we tend to look upon it as a herb, it could be considered just as a vegetable and make up a bigger part of our vegetable dietary. The stems – at their best when the plant is about to bloom – can be peeled and eaten raw in salads, or made into soups, or boiled and eaten as a vegetable. Florence fennel, another variety, is a more thick-set plant than common fennel and more productive of swollen stems. Fennel leaves have long been used for flavouring fish; this was traditional even in Culpeper's day: 'One good old Fashion is not yet left off, viz. to boil Fennel with Fish: for it consumes that Phlegmatick Humor, which Fish most plentifully afford and annoy the Body by.' Culpeper also tells us that fennel 'taketh away the Loathings'. The plant was much better known, and more used, in medieval times than it is now. Piers Plowman mentions 'a ferthyng-worth of fenel seed, for fastying dayes'. Like so many other plants it was also credited with power against a multitude of diseases, including, as so often, the bites of mad dogs. But, in the last respect, as Alphonse Karr somewhat cynically remarks in his *Voyage Autour de mon Jardin*: 'At the end of three or four hundred years it began to be seen that it had never cured anyone.' It takes a long time to disillusion the credulous.

Sow fennel, either common or Florence, in any good, well-manured soil. Sow early for it germinates slowly. The common fennel will go on growing for years; Florence fennel must be sown anew each spring.

Florence fennel

Fennel
Foeniculum vulgare

PARSNIP

Umbelliferae
BIENNIAL

'THE wild being better than the tame', says Culpeper of the parsnip, 'shews Dame Nature to be the best Physician.' He believed that both root and seed were good, among other less delicate things, for 'the Bitings of Serpents'. Lemery thought the garden parsnip was good for wounds and kept down vapours. As for Parkinson, he wrote: 'The Parsnep root is a great nourisher, and is much more used in the time of *Lent*, being boyled and stewed with butter, than in any other time of the year.' The reason it was much used in Lent was because it is one root which will stay quite happily in the ground all winter, not being destroyed by frost. In fact it is improved by frost. Tournefort noticed that in Lent 'they are the sweetest, by reason the juice has been concocted during the winter, and are desired at that season especially, both for their agreeable Taste and their Wholesomeness. For they are not so good in any respect, till they have been first nipt with Cold.' Wild parsnips grow near the sea in many parts of northern Europe. The cultivated strain was evolved from the wild ones by selection; the finest was produced by Professor Buckman between 1848 and 1850. He named it the 'Student' and it has formed the basis of most of our modern varieties, much as Cruikshank's Shorthorn has of our cattle. The Russian name for parsnip is *pasternak*.

Sow the seed in good, well-dug ground in early spring. If you sow late in the spring you will get smaller parsnips, which will be sweeter to the taste for autumn eating but less good for weathering the long winter.

Parsnip
Pastinaca sativa

PARSLEY

Umbelliferae
BIENNIAL

'THE Rootes of percelly soden tender, and made in a succade, is good for the stone, and doth make a man to pysse.' So Boorde tells us. The ancient Greeks used to sprinkle parsley on the dead. They had a saying that a person who was near to death was 'in need of parsley'. The roots of the plant were much eaten in olden times, and even the English have long cooked with the leaves. John Partridge, in his *Treasury of Hidden Secrets and Commodious Conceits* of 1586 gives this recipe for a sauce of roast rabbit apparently favoured by Henry VIII: 'Take a handfull of washed Percelly, mince it small, boyle it with butter and verjuice upon a chafing-dish, season it with suger and a little pepper grosse-beten; when it is redy put in a few crummes of white bread amongst the other: let it boyle againe till it be thicke, then laye it on a platter, like the breadth of three fingers, laye of each side one roasted conny and so serve them.' A 'conny' is a rabbit; 'verjuice' is cider vinegar, and many country people still use this name. Parsley has many country superstitions attached to it, one being that to transplant it, particularly from an old home to a new, brings bad luck. Another is that it grows better for a wicked man than for a good one: I am afraid I always get good crops.

The seeds take long to germinate – which has given rise to the belief that 'they go seven times to the Devil and back before they germinate'. To counteract this satanic connection, Good Friday is recommended as the day to sow parsley. Put plenty of humus in the soil and have patience.

[94]

Parsley
Petroselinum crispum

Common parsley

Hamburg parsley

Broad-leaved parsley

Index of Common Names

For DORLING KINDERSLEY LIMITED

Editorial Christopher Davis
Design Roger Bristow
Research Lucy Lidell